CW00421813

The Glass-Blower

OTHER BOOKS OF POETRY BY KEKI N. DARUWALLA

Under Orion (Writers Workshop, Calcutta, 1970)
Apparition in April (Writers Workshop, Calcutta, (1971)
Crossing of Rivers (OUP, Delhi, 1976)
Winter Poems (Allied Publishers, Bombay, 1979)
The Keeper of the Dead (OUP, Delhi, 1982),
winner of the Sahitya Akademi (Academy of Letters) Prize
Landscapes (OUP, Delhi, 1987),
winner of the Commonwealth Poetry Prize for Asia
A Summer of Tigers (Harper Collins, India, 1995)
Night River (Rupa Publishers, Delhi, 2000)
The Map-maker (Ravi Dayal Publishers, Delhi, 2002)
Collected Poems 1970-2005 (Penguin India, 2006)

OTHER TITLES BY KEKI N. DARUWALLA

SHORT FICTION
Sword and Abyss (Vikas, Delhi, 1979)
The Minister for Permanent Unrest
(Ravi Dayal Publishers, Delhi, 1996)
A House in Ranikhet (Rupa, Delhi, 2002)
TRAVELOGUE
Riding the Himalayas (Niyogi Books, 2006)

KEKI N. DARUWALLA
The Glass-Blower
SELECTED POEMS

PUBLICATIONS
2008

Published by Arc Publications
Nanholme Mill, Shaw Wood Road
Todmorden, Lancs OL14 6DA, UK
www.arcpublications.co.uk
Copyright © Keki Daruwalla 2008

Design by Tony Ward

Printed at Biddles Ltd.,
King's Lynn, Norfolk

ISBN 987 1904614 44 9 (pbk)
ISBN 978 1904614 80 7 (hbk)

ACKNOWLEDGEMENTS
The publishers wish to thank
Penguin India for permission to reproduce
the poems which appear in
Keki N. Daruwalla *Collected Poems (1975-2005)*
(Penguin India, 2006).

Cover image © Phoebe F. Ward, 2008

The publishers acknowledge financial
assistance from Arts Council England, Yorkshire

Arc Publications International Poets
Series Editor: John Kinsella

For
Nainaz, Freyana,
Sanaya and Shayan

Contents

from
UNDER ORION

AUTHOR'S NOTE:

The poems in my first poetry volume, *Under Orion* were written in 1968-69 in the outbacks of Barabanki, a small district town, eighteen miles from Lucknow. The poems obviously recall the era – the Beatles turning acolytes of Maharishi Mahesh, for instance.

The poem 'Pestilence' came out of sighting a patient being carried on a bed by two men in search of a village doctor, which triggered a vision of epidemics in earlier times.

Easy and Difficult Animals
for Khurshid

You have no problems such as mine,
you do not cower
from your own thoughts.
          It doesn't frighten you
the iron edge awaking from its rust
the crawl of oxidized dreams
          in lonely hours.

Where do you get your insights from
and your simple words?
Teaching our daughter that day you said
          some dreams are animals
          some dreams are birds.

The moonface was either
          turned towards light
          or away from it
dark fruit, incandescent fruit.
Your distinctions were a knife
that went cutting to the root.
You divided in two
this animal delirium that we call 'life'
into 'easy animals', 'difficult animals.'
All that moved on legs
          flew on wings
          crawled on the belly
          inhaled through fins
hedgehog and weasel and polecat
all that went to the taxidermist
marmot and buzzard and bat
you lumped together as 'easy animals'.
And pitched against this menagerie
one solitary cry
the one 'difficult animal'
that was I.

11

Pestilence

pairs of padded feet
               are behind me
astride me
               in front of me
the footpaths are black feet
converging on the town

brown shoulders   black shoulders
shoulders round as orbs
muscles smooth as river stones
                   glisten
till a dry wind scourges
the sweat from off their backs

they are palanquin-bearers of a different sort
on the string-beds they carry
no henna-smeared brides
prone upon them are frail bodies
frozen bodies   delirious bodies
some drained of fever and sap
some moving   others supine
transfixed under the sun

the hospital floors are marble white
black bodies dirty them
nurses in white habits
UNICEF jeeps with white bonnets
doctors with white faces receive them
'who says they have cholera?
they are down with diarrhoea
who says it is cholera?
it is gastro-enteritis.'

12

the land's visage is unmarked
soot-brown soot-green
                    soot-grey
mongrels tail the ambulance
till dust and gasoline fumes
choke them off

but memory like a crane arm
unloads its ploughed-up rubble
ancient visitations is what one recalls
the sweep of black feet
                    towards the ghats
dying villages
corn surplus once again
migrations as only birds have known
forgotten cattle dying at the stakes –
someone left them on tether

this is miniature by contrast
but the image lingers
string-beds creaking
over padded feet
and when of a sudden
cholera turns to death
the feet keep up their padded progress
only the string-bed is exchanged
for a plank.

Elegy I

We saw your flight bending
to a darkened skyline.

It was all so death-clear
that when it came
the simplicity of the whole thing
left us quite bewildered.

I never caught your subtler refractions.
Others saw
                    the shadows that flecked your face
                    the light that got lost in your eyes
(pardon me, the clichés are theirs).
They say now
            'She was always on the margin of things
            imagine to have died
            when she was on her way to herself.'
Even this, I being what I am,
do not understand.

Your words
and my memories of them
turn meaningless, unreal now;
your absence is so irrefutable.

There were more gestures to your hands
than I have words.
The sharpness
            in your voice
            in your finger-ends
            the tilt of the head
drove a cold wedge through our winter nights.
Your moods were hovering round
you like dark instincts.
Your death was a state of mind
before it even touched the body.

But I who saw the black snow
          flake by flake
am not so certain of things now.
A night sky will have trouble
holding on to your image
in all this sleet.
Your smile disintegrates
into a carious bowl
and as I grab at your receding words –
long, spun-out fibres , thinning into air
I feel faint and foolish
grabbing at nothing with nothing.

Collage I

Rock'n'rollers around
Ravi Shankar
scruffy hippies around Maharishi Mahesh
and Beatles around both
and we are thrilled.
They have a lot to learn
from the ragas still, these bums!
It is that same sentiment
that Tagore euphoria
after the Nobel Prize.

Since Oppenheimer quoted Bhagwad Gita
after the first A-bomb,
since Alien Ginsberg and the psychedelics
wore dhotis, and with clanging cymbals
chanted cow and Krishna
we stand bowled by Indian culture
and Indian hemp.

Who says we have done nothing?
We have abolished Zamindari
and liquor and English
and driven the whores from out the G.B. Road.

What have we forbidden
veils in front of eyes
or eyes behind veils?
We have 'inaugurated' crematoriums
with an unclaimed corpse; a V.I.P.
has opened the sluice-gates of a drain
and called it 'the drain of hope.'

Some day, here
the sun will refuse
to light the path for lepers.
In India the left hand is outcast
because it cleans the arse.

Discussing personal destiny
and collective destiny
you turn bitter.
My horoscope is only a half-truth.
Where are inflation and taxes
floor-crossing and black marketing
written in it?

If we had plague
Camus-style
and doctors searched for virus and vaccine
there would be black market in rats.

Zamindari: the zamindars were Indian rural landlords in a system devised by
the British. Zamindari was abolished in a major Act of 1950.
the G.B. Road: a street in Delhi known for its brothels.

from
APPARITION IN APRIL

Routine

The putties were left behind by the Raj,
a strip of fire round the legs in June.
Within the burning crash-helmet
the brain is a fire-pulp. The asphalt
gives way beneath our boots and sticks.
The edges of the crowd give way;
a ring of abuse re-forms behind us.
We hardly hear them for we are used to it;
their gamut ranges from 'mother-' to 'sister-seducer'.
Karam Singh marching in the same rank as I
curses under his breath,
'I have children older than them,
these kids whose pubes have hardly sprouted!'

We march to the street-crossing where young blood
fulfils itself by burning tramcars.
Beneath our khaki we are a roasted brown
but unconvinced, they wish to burn our khaki skins.
We are a platoon against a thousand.
It is all well rehearsed; a few words of warning –
A chill formality lost in fiery slogans.
'Load!' I put a piece of death up the spout.
It is all well rehearsed: I alone point
my barrel into them as I squeeze the trigger;
the rest aim into the sun.

They have gone. The Salvage Squad comes
and takes the body to the autopsy room
and tows the tramcar away.
Tension oozes out as armpits run with sweat.
Depressed and weary we march back to the Lines.
A leader says over the evening wireless,
'We are marching forward.'

Charity: Two Faces

EVANGELICAL EVA

To us black-eyed and brown-skinned
she came autumn-haired
with a jawline lost
in a pudgy, dimpled
vanilla-pudding face

True we were children
our nights aprowl with animal fables
but she had come with more exotic notions –
of serpent-lore and gourded flute
drum-gods with insidious tremors
and straw-stuffed animals
guarding the village.

Thrifty of sermon, generous with paludrine
soon she was lost in a forest of urchins
where laughter and daydreams scuttled about like birds

One evening he drove up in a yellow jeep.
He had the same flesh-tones, the same
beryl-blue eyes as hers.
A beery smile, a tottering gait
and he started banging on her timber shack
pleading with an urgency
that came from the marrow.
Her hysterics, tears didn't cut any ice.
'Keep on pimping for Christ,
little good it'll do you
you stupid bitch!' and he drove off.

Next day a village elder walked over to her
'Daughter, you surely have men
in the land you come from?
How long will you stay here
Cleaning snot from the mouths of children?'

ROTARIAN RENU

As the evening progresses
in darkening spirals
'How do you find the asparagus soup?'
she simpers
she with the long asparagus fingers.
The minutiae of words
are slurred over by coffee
a bitterness sizzling
black on the tongue
'A thousand Glaxo
baby milk tins
and ten million cc.
of penicillin
were doled out free
in Bhatinda and Jind.'
She talks on nursing
her vermouth and gin;
'a cheque for the miners
trapped in the coal
some oats for the mare
who is dropping her foals
I shouldn't be saying it
it sounds rather crude
but a thousand rupees
for the nurse who was screwed.'

Her lover is startled
he fidgets, turns red.
There's nothing the matter
why must he turn red?
Meanwhile from the platter
Salome instead
unstained, unspattered
doles out her heads.

from
CROSSING OF RIVERS

AUTHOR'S NOTE:

The poems in *Crossing of Rivers* were written
in 1972 after a stay at Benaras or Varanasi,
arguably the holiest pilgrim centre for Hindus.
Incidentally the place has been cleaned up and
no sewer flows into the Ganges now.

Boat-Ride along the Ganga

Filing into a motor boat at dusk
we scour the waters upstream.
Slowly the ghat-amphitheatre unfolds
like a nocturnal flower in a dream
that opens its petals only at dusk.
Palm-leaf parasols sprouting like freak mushrooms
brood over platforms that are empty.
Outlines blur in the winter gloom
as the *panda* points out Dasasvamedh.
I listen avidly to his legend-talk
striving to forget what I chanced to see:
the sewer-mouth trained like a cannon
on the river's flank. It is as I feared;
hygiene is a part of my conscience and I curse it
and curse my upbringing which makes me queasy here.

And while the *pandas* calculate
the amount of merit that accrues to you
at each specific ghat you cross the pyres

bowing your head to the finality of fate.
Behind the heat-haze rising from the fires,
objects shimmer, dance, levitate.
You face reality on a different plane
where death vibrates behind a veil of fire.

There is no lament. No one journeys here
to end up beating his breasts. This much the mourners learn
from the river, as they form a ring of shadows
within whose ambit flesh and substance burn.

We reverse the boat while a flight of mallard turns
and drives west into the gloom.
We move past the phantom-panorama once more,
boats ferrying sand, sailboats on anchor,
poles scattered on the river to provide some room
for birds to perch on when attacked by thirst;

and once more the pyres; against a mahogany sky
the flames look like a hedge of spear-blades
heated red for a ritual that bodes no good.
The mourners are a cave-painting, primitive, grotesque
done in charred wood.

When we disembark, the waterfront ahead
is smothered by night, red-peppered with fires
as *doms* and *mallahs* cook their unleavened bread.

Dante would have been confused here.
Where would he place this city,
in Paradise or Purgatory, or lower down
where fires smoulder beyond the reach of pity?
The concept of the goddess baffles you –
Ganga as mother, daughter, bride.
What plane of destiny have I arrived at
where corpse-fires and cooking-fires
burn side by side.

---

panda: a Hindu priest.
Dasasvamedh: a ghat named after the ten-horse sacrifices by the ancient
Bharasiva kings who bathed here after the sacrifices.
doms: funeral attendants, a caste by themselves.
mallahs: boatmen.

Dawn

Coincidence of forms along the waterfront
coincidence of silhouettes
     in the spear-grass street,
water and sky and the farther bank
breaking apart
     and rock-pigeons
that scatter like debris.
Contused purple
     turns to mauve
dragging nirvana
along the streets of dawn.
Dark olive mud, sandheads that bulge
like a herd of bison rising from their sleep.
Objects bristle with outline;
a silhouette lost in prayer
develops feet,
a frayed anchorite walks
like a fossil saint
who has crawled out
from the sediments of time.

There is a clang of cymbals
like brass beating against brass.
A conch-cry pierces the receding fog
like a shaft of light.
Gongs sound like hammered gold
and then a bald head
smeared with saffron
inching slowly above the distant reeds
dawns on the Ganga
like a bizarre illusion.

Vignette II

In the lower reaches of the sky
a lull of kites.

But along the river
you can feel the sound
    with your hands;
roll it along the mouth.
You can tell the time of the day
by it and the sharpness of frost
and whether the night was a river
    or a precipice.

Only the river doesn't speak here.
She is thought itself
a soundless interior monologue.

Tonsured heads explode along
the water surface.
All is spider-thread ritual here;
sandal-paste and mantra
chanting of the *gayatri*
shaved head and *pinddan*.

You go the rounds of the Panchtirath
starting from the ghat where Durga
had dropped a sword
to where she dropped an earring
and the Panchganga ghat where four rivers
are said to meet the Ganga,
like this river of faith going down
the stone-steps to meet the river.

Women do not take off their saris
as they enter the water;
men leave their clothes behind.
The dead leave their bodies.

Kites hang in the air
in suspended animation.
Shadows hang like birds on a dead wind.

A blind man's fingers grope across my face.
A sadhu eyes me unblinking from his navel.

---

gayatri: a sacred hymn.
pinddan: balls of rice offered to dead ancestors, and then fed to cows.
Panchtirath: stands for five sacred places. A ghat (embankment) is named
after them at Varanasi (Benares).
sadhu: a Hindu anchorite.

31

from
WINTER POEMS

Suddenly the Tree

1

While you slept and the quilt heaved
with your even breathing,
winter came like a bearded goat-herd,
armed with a crook and barefooted.
Suddenly the tree near our window shook,
its whiskers twitched,
its leaves, yellow and ochrous
like henna-smeared hands
fell severed from the wrists.
Large moth-wings struck against the window,
turned, and scraping against the wall
drifted down, wind-raked.
The tree is now all bark and bough.
Leafless twigs scratch
against the glass
like skeletal children
scribbling on a slate,
chalk-fingered.
There is a smell of hail
in the air and lightning-burns.
The just-widowed wind
beats her head against the glass panes.

2

When sand churns in its belly
the wind becomes visible.
    I can see its gesticulations
the expressions ripped away
    like torn wings,
its passions flaking off
like dandruff, like falling hair,
    like scar tissue,
the wires of grit
blown back like maenad-hair.

35

3

Last night I heard the thick waters of your dreams
lap the shores of your body.
Your frame shook, your groans
erupted from the same pit
as your cries when you climax.
I heard the thick waters of your dreams
lap the shores of your night;
behind your rhinestone eyes
flickered a flame of terror.

I shook you and brought you back
to the four walls of this room,
the night lamp, the carpet
and the crescent of my arms.

But you tucked the dream
within the sleeve of your body.
It lies coffined in your psyche now,
another seal affixed on the mouth of love.
You never opened up. You knew
a handful of your waters scooped upon my face
would scald me. Half an hour of your terrors
would haunt me for a lifetime.

Behind your rhinestone eyes
flickered compassion.

4

In twig-nested
          and sparse-leaved
November
          the nest
                    against the dusk
glowers like a
casing of charred ribs
                    bristles
as if a bush
had been
                    grafted
on a tree fork
                    bloats
as if a gland
                    in the tree's groin
had turned tumorous.
But the nest is lined
                    with cottonseed
and raffia.
Overhead the mother kite
                    keens
                    circling anxiously.
Within the twig-walls
                    fledgelings
                    shrill consonants
                    syllables.

5

The hive slept like Argus
its thousand eyes covered with bees.

The light as it fell through the neem tree
was a marine light, in which
yellow moths set sail
from one perforated shadow to another.

The hive was mystic,
a drugged mantra
with its dark syllables asleep.
As the afternoon wore on
the honey-thieves came
and smoked the bees out
and carved out a honey-laden
crescent for themselves
and left a lump of pocked wax behind.

The bees roamed the house,
too bewildered to sting the children.
At night they slept, clinging
to the tree fork, now scarred with burns.

Sparrows and squirrels, a bird
with a black crest and a red half-moon
for an eyelid bickered over
the waxed remains the next day.
Then with a drone of straining engines
the bees rose like a swarm of passions
from a dying heart, and left.

6

Red in the eye of the sun,
(spatter of haemoglobin)
shadow-singed and dark-petalled
in the shade, the poppy flares.

This is not the poppy I am used to.
I have seen fields, flowering white,
stretching into horizons of dust,
the pod of the poppy when raked,
oozing white elixir that turned brown.

And I remember the one-eyed carrier
with his shaggy nag,
and the dust-coated cabs
waiting on canal roads
to cart the opium.

But this is different,
this kindled match-head in the underbrush,
this globe of fire
near the ferned waterhole.
A bee, lost in the
silken scrolls of its petals,
moves towards the core
of this little world – dark amnesia
ringed with fiery blood.
This is the wine going to the head,
the arterial throb
at the pierced heart of nature.

7

We have come of age:
>   those who grew up with us
>   have already started dying.
Now is the need felt
for a membrane, firstly,
>   to intervene at the border
>   where love meets love.
We have to come unstuck, we need
something to make the crossroads less cruel,
>   something to hold back
>   the seething tide of memory
as it sulks and snags so that it
eddies back into a quiet abeyance.
>   Gestures must peel off like hot
>   red petals from a green stem.
And this grudging acceptance
from the heart we need –
>   like glutinous milk from the lanced poppy –
>   that nothing, but nothing belongs to us.
Let's adjust to shifts of light and shifts of shadows
We have come of age
>   the dreams which grew up with us
>   have already started dying.

Calendar, Starting with June

It is equal to living in a tragic land
To live in a tragic time.
Wallace Stevens

1

They sprained their necks looking up for clouds,
the light so harsh that corneas
started smoking at the edges.

First the clouds flashed past like migratory birds.
Then in answer to some unheard utterance
from the parched lips of this land
they settled like birds come to roost.

All the accessories were here, humidity, loam,
wet earth-odours – everything except rain.

The black buck got its coat in September, the sun
came out so sharp and stinging.

Never was the harvest moon clearer – a bloated,
well-fed, muskmelon.

The sky an intense blue, the stars
lighted ulcers on the sky's belly.

December dust haze. Cold turning grey.
A sky of bone.

January, still rainless, and the temperature
sinking like a cement sack
hitting the lake bed.

Frost, and in the shrinking *jheels*
the water-hiccup of the lake fish

as they moved under the moss. Wind,
and the fledgeling grain scattered on the earth.

March – hail, and the last glimpse of a lean Orion
as he tightens his belt
around his emaciated waist.

The April wind, hyena-mouthed,
goes for the mango blossom.

Wind turning fiery over scar-tissue land.
Animal tongues hang out. A woman ends her
thirst in a dry well, one babe in each armpit.

2

From the dusk of the foothill pines,
long-shadowed and clear,
I walk downhill
to the dusk of thickets,
short and stubbed
and frazzled with the cry of jackals.

The shrillness of pine-crickets,
the crackle of locusts being fried,
is gone – Instead a nightjar works through the night
like a pebble bouncing
along an icebound gradient.

Dawn:
the land, hard as rigor mortis,
flowering with bone-bush.

The ribs prominent:
latitudes running around the body-map.
Ribs prominent:
had there been flesh or skin
to encase them
you could have used the rib-bowl
to draw water from a well –
had there been water in the well.

3

A hot wind throws
scabs of this once living river
into your sunstruck face,
as you traverse the bridge,
pylon after pylon
over a river of sand,
a swathe of iron filings in the sun.

The land is an earthen dish,
empty as always,
baked and fired in a cosmic kiln,
There are smithy-fires overhead –
they are forging another sky!
The coppersmith bird shrieks insistent
that death is round the corner.
The gulmohar coughs blood,
the sagun leaves turn a warped bronze.
Only the blind koel, the stupid koel
talks of rain in the mango grove.

Hope is a diseased kidney
which has already been removed.
The monsoons won't arrive.
They have forgotten to board the ship.

This is it
the last summer of our despair,
the inner desert shuffling across
with skeleton arms
to meet the outer desert.

Author's note: This poem has a stanza on each of the twelve months in the calendar. They were written during the drought of 1975-76 and the massive drought of 1979.
jheels: a sort of shallow lake.
gulmohar: a flowering tree, 'flamboyant'.
koel: the Indian blackbird, whose call is supposed to foreshadow rain.

Notes

A bread-bus halts
Its bumper and mudguard
              are delicious.

Selling kerosene to a crowd:
how aesthetic
the flame that rides the street.

No end to hoarding.
Breaking open the lockers they find
a briefcase full of rice.

A child tucked in each armpit
she jumps into the well –
her husband had run away with their last meal.

First utensils, then silver anklets,
lastly cattle. A pregnant cow
was sold for seven millet cakes.

There is no red-light area in the town
where starving daughters can be sold.
The river bank comes to the rescue,
              its sand soft as volcanic ash.

Rhapsody on a Hungry Night

We move to Satara
Gulbarga, Goalpara?
Or some place in Sahara
several nightmares
removed from reality.

We are moving in freight cars
loaded with rice stocks.
This is our mandate,
no food bandit
must get near the freight cars.
At wayside flag stations
profiteers offer us
ten thousand per wagon.
Waif women are offered
one buck for a roll.

Instead of water
splashed shades of the jujube;
Instead of crops
crab grass and fern.
We'll match other planets
crater for crater
as we move to the outer
membranes of the finite,
as we move towards
the gouged face of the moon.

What place are we going to?
What deserts of reason,
stretch upon arid stretch,
where one side harangues
'Democracy in danger!
The men are corrupt!
So forget your vocations
Take a one-year holiday
and go for them hard.'

And the others declaim
'Democracy in danger!
The Plan is in danger!
Foreign hand in all this!
It's despair that will kill you
not a shortfall in vitamins.
So look out for hope.'

Sheep are looking for green words
on the dry page of the earth.

We move from Satara
(Gulbarga? Goalpara?)
Or some place in Sahara
several realities
removed from a nightmare.

The Wringing of Hands

News came from the coast, fifty miles away
his wife's cousin was missing. He was free
and lucky – there was no paddy to transplant,
nor daughter to marry and shift
from one mud patch to another.

He walked over land dry enough to set fire to.
Hard enough to crucify a god on.
Cracks wide enough to swallow a million Sitas.

A dark speck, his legs scissoring the distance
he caterpillared across the riven land.
A lost gull, the tang of a south-easter,
and salt dunes told him he was near;
and then the low thunder of the surf.
Against the line where sea and sky
met, wringing their blue-veined hands,
he saw tin-and-tar shacks, roach-quick
and the dog's tongue of the sea lolling;

His nephews sat skull-cropped,
their necks vein-corded, their heads
bandaged with resignation.
Everywhere he saw haunted looks, the same
fears fermenting in salt-rot bodies,
old matchstick bones groaning
under the gnarled hide. They were not meeting
on fissured land or the fissured coast.
They were meeting in the marshes of hunger.

An oil slick's dribble had wandered here
right into the sea's cradle. It cleaned up
the oyster-beds and looked under
the coral-drapes for hiding children.
Fish bobbed up, lead grey, sturgeon grey.
Whatever came in the crook of its soft, smooth, arm
turned belly up in the brown wash of the sea.

48

Some iron tentacle was bending both
the Barley God and the Sea God to its dark will.

Life scuttled further into the sea,
far from the rheumy death that lined the coast.
Whatever turned up in the meshes stank
till villages inland refused to dole out cash
for dinghies mortgaged or daughters pawned.

His wife's cousin had hoisted sail.
'I will go to the heart of the sea
and bring it back' he had said.
No one knew what the old man meant.
He wouldn't take anyone with him,
not friend nor nephew. There was more to this
than mere fishing. He had challenged
the death that pulsed in the waters,
and a shoal of myths already thrashed
around his dinghy. He had great faith
in her timber and her stump of a mast.
Nudged by an offshore wind,
it cut the water like a fin,
right to the shark waters from where the fish had fled.
A day, a night, another day and still
no fish, and then the sweats broke.
His heart heaved and strained like a hooked fish
and stumbled into a murmurless quiet.

Two days, and the boats set out for him,
facing the unblinking scrutiny of the sea
and the sun which stared
from the dead belly of the waves.
The gulls with their black-stud eyes
followed the boats. Another day, and they saw
the stump of a mast, the dinghy ghosting,
and the uncle reclined against the stern,
his shirt collar flapping in the wind.

Silently they prayed and turned the boat shorewards.
It was then the fish broke its still cover
and threshed and tugged at the hooked
bit of death inside its throat.
The line jumped as he fought the curved barb
inside his thorax, and thrashed against the water.
And they sailed into the village with nine feet
of spine and blubber and fin
and the impassive eyes of a saint.

It was the first live catch in two months.
Death was poling away from the coast
and the waters would be clear.
Beneath the cropped skulls of his nephews
he discovered the first stirrings
among the black roots of hope.
After the death-feast he said to them
even as he packed his few things in his bag
'We are going to live here
(Where else could the bugger go?)
We are going to live right here
under this blue bowl of the sky,
this bowl filled
with a million tomorrows.'

'Cracks wide enough to swallow a million Sitas': Sita, daughter of mother earth and wife of the legendary King Rama, appealed to "the Earth-goddess to rebut the charge of unfaithfulness made against her. This the Earth-goddess did by emerging from the earth, seated on a golden throne, and by embracing Sita and disappearing with her into the earth from which she had miraculously sprung." (From A *Dictionary of Hinduism* by Margaret and James Stutley).

Variations

Sandbag on sandbag
the wall of the dead rises.
Today hunger is forbidden,
tomorrow food.
At noon silence was taboo –
you must be social, converse, smile,
show that there is no terror around.
At night speech was forbidden:
you've no right to disturb others.
Especially forbidden were noisy dreams.
Dream on dream,
corpse on corpse
the wall of the dead rises.

It is over now;
there is no point ringing for the doctor
Ring for the undertaker
the mortician
the caretakers of the Nigambodh Ghat.

On a moist window
I make an eyehole
with the ball of my finger.
But when I look out there's nothing
nor wind nor trees nor grass.

The blind also gaze
unseeing out of windows.
The crowd wipes the moisture from the pane,
looks at me
and finds nothing there.
Thus the world and I
stand across a moist
window pane
the unreal looking at the unreal.

Everything turns inwards.
You scratch a windowpane
with a bird-claw and it turns
into a mirror at night.
Never was awareness
more intense. Shadows
have taken shelter
in the creases of your face.
Outside, the fervent, narrow
streets of certainty
lead to the clock tower
which booms
with rhetorical flourishes.
The mirror only speaks
of warped interiors,
wobbling frontages.

Stone jars with mango pickle
bottles red with chilli powder
stacks of old newspapers
looking like a block of unresilient rubber.
A spool of thread,
dust on the stone shelves
and a mousetrap
its teeth rusty, yet poised
for the kill.
A splinter of bread
that looks like a dead tongue.
There are no windows, no
skylights; everywhere mousetraps.
Things crawl, scurry, serrate.
The place is agog with eyes –
holes drilled in the darkness
and stuffed with malevolent jelly.

Everything is in place,
the prisoner in his night suit
still fighting his hangover,
the hurriedly passed statute,
the assize assembled through
staff cars and printed invitations.
Everything gazetted, notified
passed by the finance,
endorsed by the Law Ministry.
This is order,
the corpse and the coffin-maker
at their appointed places.

They shake their heads and say
'we want evidence'.
How can I explain
that there cannot be any evidence.
For when the state rapes
the streets are empty.

Author's note: This is a poem on the draconian Emergency promulgated in 1975
by Prime Minister Indira Gandhi on a hapless country.

from
THE KEEPER OF THE DEAD

The Revolutionary

It had never come
burning across his skin
like a hot dye.
And yet he shook, a leaf in the wind,
sweated like the floor-plinth of a stalactite
at the mere thought of it,
a lash-burn smoking on his back.

As a schoolboy when, hoodlums
had mugged a friend of his
with cycle-chains,
bystanders, when the show was over,
splashed water on his face and not his friend's
for shock had turned to hard ice on his brow.

And now lean and volatile and so intent
that half a life seemed packed in every gesture,
and so young, who would have thought
that death sat on his vulture-shoulders?

This was the time, he thought, this
when dry dusk followed dry dawn
in the second year of the drought;
this was the time,
when tongues were hanging out
like red wounds
that they should strike the match
with all that dry-as-death driftwood
waiting for the spark!
Revolution!
The road of flame!

What hawk would wheel in
with the message tagged to the claws:
'Let shells rain on the Drought-City,
mobilize despair and turn it to murder!
Put the city to torch! Let it not thrive on shame –
our staple diet!'

One morning, posters
grew out of walls like fungus,
the bald head of a statue rolled,
face smeared with tar,
a flame-thrower fell on a police outpost
blinding a recruit in one eye.

They nabbed him at three in the morning,
cosy in his quilt,
and dreaming of his mother,
his unkempt handsomeness
in disarray around him –
and wildly stammering.

Were these the tumbrils rolling,
roles reversed, the bourgeois throng
screaming for blood?
Was that woman standing on the balcony,
rocking in lament, his mother?
And the younger one who couldn't afford to cry
whose face crumpled only in the bathroom –
was that his girl?
They took him to a room where the stones
were as damp as his brow,
where the lash dangled from a rusty peg
and he shivered – from cold or fear or both, I cannot say.

And far into the night, as Orion crashed
groundwards, a shadow
that fell tree-like across his cell,
was that the angel of death
or a lawyer wringing his hands
pleading for bail?

The Mistress

No one believes me when I say
my mistress is half-caste. Perched
on the genealogical tree somewhere
is a Muslim midwife and a Goan cook.
But she is more mixed than that.
Down the genetic lane, babus
and professors of English
have also made their one-night contributions.

You can make her out the way she speaks;
her consonants bludgeon you;
her argot is rococo, her latest 'slang'
is available in classical dictionaries.
She sounds like a dry sob
stuck in the throat of darkness.

In the mornings her mouth is sour
with dreams which had fermented during the night.
When I sleep by her side
I can almost hear the blister-bubble
grope for a mouth through which to snarl.
My love for her survives from night to night,
even though each time
I have to wrestle with her in bed.

In the streets she is known.
They hiss when she passes.

Despite this she is vain,
flashes her bangles and her tinsel;
wears heels even though her feet
are smeared up to the ankles with henna.

She will not stick to *vindaloo*, but talks
of roasts, pies, pomfrets grilled.
She speaks of cointreau and not cashew
arrack which her father once distilled.

No, she is not Anglo-Indian. The Demellos would
bugger me if they got scent of this,
and half my body would turn into a bruise.
She is not Goan, not Syrian Christian.
She is Indian English, the language that I use.

The Night of the Jackals

1

It is just the telephone between us,
grey, impersonal:
'The children are sleeping,' she says, 'Come!'
She had to think of me now
with the elements in full cry
and the air smelling of lightning-burns
like a scorched pelt!

I park my car eleven blocks away.
People scurry off the roads
          as the sky crackles,
I press the buzzer hard
and tap at the glass door
along with the thunder.
Tonight she will be waiting
arched fully backwards
vibrant as new leaf!
She sits there, white cardigan, dark slacks,
laughing, as she knits away
caressing the rug with her bare feet.

The blankets over her children
heave with their regular breathing.
It will go well with her
if I kiss them on their foreheads.
          Suddenly
she is in my arms
          swarming.

Her nipples and the grass outside
harden together,
tense with coming thunder.
Kissing her on the neck
I nibble the words
as they slur across her skin:
did the thunder frighten you?

Yes, with both the kids asleep
it was eerie, terrifying.
And if the children had been awake
she may not have thought of me
          for another three months!
As if in reply
she presses me harder to herself.
I enter her
the way a boat starved of fresh water
enters a harbour.

2

Dust spurts as
the first rains come
gaunt and spindly.
'Winter was dying,'
she says, shivering
'till this…'
pointing to the drip outside.
Near my village, in the foothills
it must have hailed,
killing the mango blossom.

But July, you must come then!
There is a different feel about things –
the earth oozing with black treacle,
fat grubs, white
          as intestinal shreds,
fireflies like blood-cells of the night;
even the hiss of the scythe
in the wet grass
is different!

When I tread the leaf-mould,
and the soot-black earth
gives way under bare feet
then alone I feel
I have not been carved out
of a patch of dried blood.'
Why not go in the rains then?
'Not in the rains,' she said,
'by no means in the rains!
What will the women say?
The bleached woman has come back
          to the green grasses!'

3

Through the night we
          drift apart
and drift into each other.
Overhead the night roars.
Our blood soars and jack-knifes,
burns and then drifts away
on the cry of a bird.

Next morning she is a coriander leaf
          newly plucked,
rain-washed.
A feeling leafs, branches out
like a baby arm
across the webbing that cocoons my ribs;
a feeling softer than skull-membranes.
And I reach over for her
soft and willing and naked
and slowly rhythmic.

The toddlers are around now
or I would have rested
my head on your thighs
and buried my face
in your soft belly.

Whence this ache in the eyelids,
the forehead, the lips, this
sudden ache for being belly-smothered?
I close my eyes and dream the moment away
this flash-flood in the veins for you,
          you, soft and yielding.

4

In the afternoon I am alone
with beer and salted snacks –
she is busy with the children.
The hail cannonades on the roof-tiles,
and then the wildcat wind.
It is now that the spasm gets her:
cough and sputum
and even a little blood.

'In our village, the wind
is not a beggar,' she says.
'It comes riding on the hooves
of wild horses
or shrilling on the cry of a bird.
Not like an *Agori*, gritty and alone
while children watch
cowering from the windows.'

'Let's go,' she said, 'I'll park
the children with my cousin.
Let's go!
The place must be ablaze now,
the bougain swarming
over the roof!
The semul tree!
The flame of the forest!'

5

This, she said, was the well of the goddess –
but if it was the well of the goddess
the rust on this Persian wheel
would have been temple *bhog* by now;
and these hooded oxen
ploughing through eternity,
round the well, circumambulating,
they would have stored merit enough
to be gods in the next birth!

But as a shadow drifted across her brow
she added, which heaven can afford
a million kine-gods?

6

'When the semul tree
flowers with embers
that's the time the cough gets me.
It's the flower-dust, I think.'
'Pollen', I corrected her
and read dismay in her eyes.
'How will you ever write, my love!
Poetry is written with
the wrong words, don't you know?'

7

The jackals sink their fangs
into the veins of the night.

Their cries herald
the death of the wilderness
the passing of ghosts.

I look for hairline
fractures on the glass panes
as the wail of the jackals,
riding the wind
crackles against the windows.

For a moment I am amazed
that the almond tree
all dressed up in white
does not sway on its black roots
in the wail and the wind
of these vulpine hungers;
but stands there petrified,
a white shadow
etched on the darkness,
its white flowers tattooed
on the body of the night.

8

In March, the women say, 'A spirit
inhabits her.
Don't you see the flush spreading
like bracken fire on her cheeks?'

And I tell them I am not
a vine that starts leafing
only in spring.
Whenever you are near me I flower.

9

The wind outside is still
and shadows freeze like dogs
awaiting their master's commands.
For an hour now the cough
has shrilled and rasped around her
like a jackal-pack.
When I can stick it no more
I take her in my arms.
The cough does not subside
but she says: 'One day
I'll die like this,
on your shoulder, coughing!'
Shadows come scrambling back, although
the branches of the semul tree
do not move across the window.
Have I a touch of the acid-god?
One month with me, and she is
already talking of dying!

Agori: a sect, among sadhus, not exactly known for its personal hygiene.
bhog: sacramental food.

From the Snows in Ranikhet
To a friend newly married

Words, footholds, winds, are trapped in the snow here
a little effort and they can be found.
Just dig through two white feet of silence
till you hit the ground.
Even now the hush is where it was
when the flakes first floated down.

Branches span out in spiked gestures
framed against the skies.
Their skeleton fingers burn with frost.
But vengeance still is Christ's –
each night frost like a murdered stiff
is stretched upon the ice.

But the goddess of the seasons
still chews her cosmic cud.
Her mastication brings forth
green leaf and golden bud,
Fish will erupt from larval beds
and go downstream with the flood.

The earth will speak, it has to.
Thaw with his unseen plough,
will trek the undercrust, expose
the vast, germinal slough.
Spring with her flaring grass-skirt
will come and take her bow.

It's a pleasant thought that seasons
will in each other blend
while you move along a landscape
of yearning that will end
in the precincts of your bodies
which you'll seed and tear and rend.

And heal with your own bodies;
that is the crux of love:
the falcon-fury of the moment
turns into the dove.
The face as spirit, the face as flesh
blend in the face as love.

You'll be probing for the fire-core
of creation subtly red,
the embryo hatched from your joint flame.
Yet don't forget the dead;
for you'll do a little killing
with every act in bed.

Old terrors that were sung of
even in ancient runes
will die a cell-by-cell death
within your bed and soon
you will explore dead cities
in each house of the moon.

But let us keep it level
and keep singing of desire.
The earth is waiting keenly
to hear your spirit singing,
to hear your bodies singing,
a duet on fire.

The Parsi Hell

The Parsi hell is insubstantial; a long
stint in the house of falsehood, foul food
and speech turning base on a wailing tongue.

Even the Chinvat Bridge which turns its edge
towards the evil is not an Aztec knife
which cuts through fat, spliced tendon, cartilage.

It is allegorical, a bridge you cannot cross
in your quest for the region of endless lights.
In the *gathas* there is nothing gross;

just one material reference – the darkness
is so thick you can cut it with a knife.
No other hells confront you in their rancour.

Our hell and heaven have no locus, the scriptures forego
all reference to the damned. The three-fold dark
is hinted at, and a passing mention of the states of woe.

Standing at the dark heart of my dreams,
the small change of guilt turning sweaty in my hands,
I watch my slow surrender at the seams,

the thread showing through frayed edges. Desires
fester in the body's abscessed tabernacles.
Like a fire temple I hoard my inner fires,

hoard my semen, brown with inbreeding. Genetic rust?
I carry within me the city of faith
desiccated with the salts of lust.

Death hums over the wires: what afflicts the spawn
is rickets, polio, a drug gone rogue. Daughters
walk out on the tribe. The forepaws

of wilderness reach for the heart. Anxieties congregate
and claw at your dreams as they prospect for hell.
You will cross the hump and come to terms with fate

as you wind up naked at the dakhma well.
Burdens vary. Throughout life a man carries his death
even as a woman carries her child.

A Parsi carries his hell.

Chinvat Bridge: this has to be crossed by all the souls after death. It turns into
a sword-edge for the unrighteous who are thus unable to cross it.
gathas: sacred hymns attributed to Zoroaster.
dakhma: Tower of Silence
Author's note: The Parsis, the people to which I belong, follow the teachings
and faith of Zarathushtra (Zoroaster). We came by boat to Gujarat from Iran
in the eighth century, fleeing from Arab persecution and forcible conversion
to Islam. The Parsis today are diminishing at a fast rate. One of the causes for
their numerical decline is sterility brought about by generations of inbreeding.

To My Daughter Rookzain

Three years and then again
the uterus flowered.

Lights reeled for her
and then blacked off
as they drew you
from the weedbed of the womb.

Then you cried:
a lung of light
in a dark room
and she came back.

Two vaccine-marks
sprout bulbous on your arm
which lies over my shoulder
halfway across my back,

and as you turn warmer
and heavier in my arms
I know that sleep has caught up with you.

Supple-boned fledgeling
you are all gristle, soft-chalk bone
and spiny shadow,
your looks quick with startled birds.

Snug in a forest of syllables
without which the winds prowl
without which the winds howl
        but cannot enter.

May you live for ever
        in the house of words.

But if you falter, blind with rain
don't panic, you'll find an arm
brown as bark
and when you reach for the bark
may you find the flowers thereon.

While wandering you may hitchhike
through the strangest lands
but when you rest
have known things around you.

Look fresh, like a rain-washed leaf
with a spray of light on it
and may your breath be spiked
as now, with the tang
of mint and clove and cinnamon.

The Mazars of Amroha
For Nandan and Latika

THE SCORPION MAZAR

Just a cluster of domes; and on ledge and parapet
dove-siesta. Even bluebottles, drongoes
failed to bring colour to this heart-grey landscape.
The cold afternoon was hammered out of zinc.

This was no *dargah* where *qawwals*
exercised their lungs at night
and royalty came barefoot
asking for son or kingdom.
Just a tree that spiralled out of a grave,
a wall on which Shah Vilayat had 'travelled'
to welcome an incoming anchorite;
and the tombs where people brought dough-lumps
to feed sick cattle after the dough was blessed.

It was the scorpions who were on display here,
their menace for ever frozen.
Whisked out of a matchbox one slid across my palm
with a spider's lichened touch,
like an acrobat walking on his hands.

'Thou shall not sting', were the saint's last words.
Are they scorpions or ascetics, these black ones
these iron-grey ones who have
excised their sting at a command
and denied their passions, as they kept
to themselves each drop of deliberate venom?

Who are the fakirs here?
the ones who sleep
or the ones who crawl?

The Coming of the Sufi

It was winter when he crossed the river.
The cotton tree was in flower and the wind
was full of the dove-grey fluff of the plumed grass.
As he squelched through mud-islands, gull-marked,
geese and mallard rose –
a screaming island seemed to rise on wings!

He walked through a dawn of marsh-birds
and wastes of plumed grass till he reached
fields spiked with scarecrows, fields of mustard
where nights resounded to the peasant's din
as they shooed boar and porcupine away.

Some miles away from the town he shacked up
in a guava-grove. And disciples gathered
fungus-like around him; and each day they came
to him at dusk after he had turned to the Kaaba.
For though the wind showed fangs
Nasiruddin's heart glowed like a lantern.

One day a disciple of Shah Vilayat
brought him a clay urn full of milk;
Nasiruddin placed a rose in the milk-urn
and returned it to the Pir.

The acolytes asked what this sign-talk was about
and he answered, 'The milk-urn, was sent to show
the chalice was full!
The town already had a saint!

Where was the room for me in Amroha?
So I placed a rose in the urn
a child-skin rose without thorns.

I would live here like a flower!
Without trespass, without encumbrance!

75

Nasiruddin Rides a Tiger

The season turned, and the flame of the forest
flowered with embering coals.
The koel cried in the mango-groves
the crickets shrilled through the night.
But the flag of his hopes flew at half-mast.
True, they honoured him, a fisherman
would bow as he passed by; a keeper
of melon-beds would pour the dust he trod
over his bald head, dark as pumpkin gourd.

But where was the ring of disciples
the ecclesiastical debates on vision
and alchemy, being and non-being, the homage
from muezzins, maulvis, the divines?

Nasiruddin chafed; his ambition was obvious
like antennae, probosces. Who knew when
the arm of god, outstretched in blessing, withdrew;
when his visions, an overhang of light, collapsed
and when the brainfires would gutter.

'Bring me a tiger!' he cried, and through his mystic powers
a tiger came. And he mounted it
and said, 'Come! let's go to the casbah!'

The Battle of Curses

And when Shah Vilayat heard that a fakir
was coming to Amroha riding on a tiger –
some upstart sufi who lived with the marsh-birds
some locust-eater thrown up by the night –
he sat astride a wall and cried, 'Move.
Let's go and receive Shah Nasiruddin!'

They met like horsemen tilting in the sun
the thin anchorite on a bounding tiger
the well-fed saint on a moving wall!
Each saw that the other had drunk
heavily from the chalice of the spirit.
Both were afraid their anger may course through
like water over a breached dam.
But it was hot, the landscape was a burnt umber
and winds sounded like an orchestral wail.

Nasiruddin, smarting, was the first to curse,
'May scorpions prowl around your grave.'
And Shah Vilayat bowed, knowing behind each word
were acres of silence. But he took
the bite out of the curse, saying,
'Yes, but the scorpions will not sting!'

Now it was Shah Vilayat's turn
and he swung the heavy mace of his curse and cried,
'Asses will roll on your grave!'
Stricken, the anchorite replied,
'Yes, but the area will be free from their turd.'

So the scorpion glides along the palm, spider-soft
and if an ass is missing in the surrounding hamlets
the owners know where to find it.

---

mazar: shrine, tomb.
dargah: a Muslim shrine.
qawwals: professional singers.
Kaaba: the holiest shrine of Muslims in Mecca.
Pir: holy man.

from
LANDSCAPES

Mandwa

Mostly when I arrive at places
it is winter. Here it isn't.
The sea pants, the islands smoulder,
the sun is an egg-yolk frying in the sky.
I have come here not to slake the senses
but to assuage an old thirst for the sea.
So to this anointed strip of coast,
dark with shrub,
the beach white with fish-scales,
girdled by islands that seem to float
like pieces of a broken carafe.

Slack surf, the tides
withdrawn into their private limbos.
Hotter than the sun
is its reflection in the sea.
Obsessive whiteness:
lime-washed shacks gleam in the afternoon.
The wavebands of the sea shimmer as we swim,
our landmark on the beach
a rusted anchor –
the spiked mace of a drowned sea god.
Neither to the shore
nor to the deep sea drag me.
Leave me here among the shoals,
anchored.

At night the harbour lights
outflicker the stars.
The wind wheezes in through shuttered slats
as if a lung of the night
were pierced by a glass sliver.

The night passes in baby-whale talk,
a baby whale which came in
with the foam and outstank the city,
till the fire-brigade cut it up
and threw it back into the ocean.

When you come to the sea
your nightmares have to adjust.
Don't look out for the flying fox,
nor wolf nor hyena;
but piranhas, bluebottles, sharks
and the bleeding blubber of dismembered whales.

Rearrange your private hells,
switch your sandstorms off
as you lock up your deserts
and bolt the skyline hard.
Clothe yourself in the limp sail
of a boat stranded in mid sea
with no fresh water.

At night I dream of an engine groaning
as it comes heavily to life:
the whisper of a force six
gusting to seven as it bellows into power.
A fistful of wind smacks the sail;
the mast cants
water churns and gurgles along the hull;
the helmsman on the wheel;
the salt, the spray, the braced legs
and the blood coursing
to a true thresh to windward.

Morning: islands, like somnambulists
which had walked out on the mainland
and awoke to find themselves
waist-deep in the seas.
The wind
        sings at
high
tide,
the palm-fronds reverberate.

Bombay is black yeast
from here, and black salt,
a wall of rotting muscle.
Across the harbour the vertical
city of the rich keeps rising –
grotesque heads on unsteady shoulders.
The slum-city of asbestos
squats at its ankles,
huddled behind a smokestack.

Horse-shaped clouds are sniffing at the sky
and whinnying, as the wind
gathers her skirts and takes off.
The jetty cannot tame the sea:
a ten-foot wall of water
with a three-foot ridge of foam
heaves against the dyke.

At night the cyclone
is many-throated, many-lunged.
Gulls dash against the lighthouse
on the hill: squall-debris.
The searchlight is hinged to a broken joint.
It swings, throwing its yellow spray
at the storm,
even though salt-blinded;
a wild dilated eye to which
birds home with wild dilated eyes.

I felt cheated in the morning,
No canting masts, no shattered spars
cluttered the beach. I had slept through
half the storm, equanimous as Buddha.
I should have dreamt
of blood-red sails, sunken ships
twisted, skeletal ghost-sailors
dropping from bits of rigging,
and eye-sockets

turning into an hourglass.
In the meadows of love
crowbar and crucifix,
the beat of death
in the flowering heart of life.
Sea, I look for fungus and rot
even in you, your floorboards putrefying
till ocean and underworld are one.

Instead, two mornings later,
this 180 degree arc
of rose and mauve,
this fleet of dawns weighing anchor.
The sea and the sky, two concaves
mirroring each other,
two giant wings of a purple moth,
a rose-pink oar looking for a boat,
a lilac axe-blade looking for a treeline.
The gulls were not there
nor their cries
nor the lazy rhythm of their wings.

I ask the villagers, surely some sea-myth
must have latched itself to this coastal shelf,
some octopus-king gliding
through palaces of luminous coral;
stories of piracies perhaps,
of a Zamorin dropping anchor.
Surely there must have been a temple here
to a fish-eyed goddess
covered with barnacles?

No, they shake their heads, no one remembers
seeing a myth die
amidst a shoal of dancing bubbles.
Nothing here but the colossal
undulations of the sea,
changing from green to shimmering jade.

Mandwa: coastal village near Bombay.
Zamorin: the name given by the Portuguese to the Kings of Calicut. This is
the King whom Vasco Da Gama first called on.

Gulzaman's Son

Climbing his tortuous way from Kanzalwan,
Gulzaman leaves the river, buckwheat harvests
and slopes dark with conifers. His breath comes
in a half-choked whistle, the air uncertain
whether to burst through the lungs, or whoosh
    out of the mouth.

He doesn't remain with his people now,
among the sheepfolds and high-pasture huts.
They rag him, 'Gulzaman, where is the son?
Can we help?' 'Here comes the randiest ram
in the valley!' They're not funny, these jibes
at his virility. So each sundown he leaves
for the river to sleep in a stone-breaker's
pine-hut, till at dawn the sheep call him.

Gulzaman strains up the last hundred feet
to reach the fold. Expectant ewes
seek shelter from the wind under the lee
of limestone walls. He sees his kinsmen,
bearded and gaunt and broad-boned as himself,
brooding over a dead kid. Rain starts hissing.
There has been such heavy sleet the week past
that in the sheepfolds new-borns have been dying.
With the mothers wind-weakened and fed
on wet grass, the lambs are still-born, flopping
inert on the earth. Ewes don't even lick
them and probe for hidden embers of life
with their raking tongues. Broken, they turn
on their sides like sacks of crushed ice.

The turf is sodden but his own fold
is a small den made snug by bales of hay.
His ewe snuggles up to him and bleats
recognition, a thin tremolo of love
blanketed by gutturals of pain.
Relations crowd, darkening the doorway,
as with heavily-greased arms Gulzaman

examines her. Yes, the lamb is on its way!
An hour later it is there, quavery-legged
and wet and uncertain about
its rickety, four-pronged hold on the earth.
Shortly it pees. Allah be praised, now it will live.
It cannot die of a chill in the stomach.
Either the doorway has been cleared, or clouds
have been parted for an instant by the sun.
Gulzaman picks the dun-coloured lamb and holds
it to his chest. 'This', he says, 'this is my son.'

Lambing

My back against the straw rick
I rest in the lambing pen,
listening to cows cudding in the dark,
their tails swishing against the buzzing flies.

I lie still, knowing pain is next door.
The lamb is already knocking at the gates,
kicking away, impatient to shift
from the pastures of my body
to the bales of hay and my warm flank.

Green grasses and clovers were aplenty here;
but I was driven to meadows
sparse and brown.
His crook prodded me,
his throwing-stick stood poised,
His shaggy dogs with their hair-screened eyes
growled when I dragged my feet.
I was herded into the sere,
into meadows dung-scabbed,
gnawed half-way to the root,
or past scythed fields
where knees bled
from the razor-cuts of stubble.

We would die of bloat, he said,
if we fed on clovers.
The stomach would turn;
thyme-scented turf was not for the likes of us.

I know of failing strength and faltering feet.
I know I am hungry but I cannot eat,
for though I am patient
the lamb within me has turned urgent
as it twists and strains against my side
and turns as I turn against the straw rick.

The smell of roasts drifts across my nostrils.
(My first-born had vanished
when his prodigal returned.)
The shepherd's hearth is warm
his cooking pot is full
the smoke from his chimney wreathes the valley.
Next morning
downs silvered with the last frosts
and the ice at the river's edge
glittering like crushed glass;
the lamb at my side licked clean;
I nibble on dry grass
unleavened with the night dews.
The green-sprout days
will shortly sun the lamb.
The Lord is my shepherd;
I shall not want.

Wolf

Fire-lit
half silhouette and half myth
the wolf circles my past
treading the leaves into a bed
till he sleeps, black snout
on extended paws.

Black snout on sulphur body
he nudged his way
into my consciousness.
Prowler, wind-sniffer, throat-catcher,
his cries drew a ring
around my night;
a child's night is a village
on the forest edge.

My mother said
his ears stand up
at the fall of dew
he can sense a shadow
move across a hedge
on a dark night;
he can sniff out
your approaching dreams;
there is nothing
that won't be lit up
by the dark torch of his eyes.

The wolves have been slaughtered now.
A hedge of smoking gun-barrels
rings my daughter's dreams.

Migrations

You don't have people now
who can sense a drought
from the way frost crinkles
on the ground in February,
a leaf leans into the wind,
or the miasmal drift
of plume-grass or burst bulrushes.
Hence this surprise today
at the tracery of earth-cracks
seen through blackened stubble.

It was sixty years back, and I a child,
terrified, as he stood at our door,
tribal-dark and thick-lipped.
God had riveted his bones well,
for they didn't fall apart,
ankle, knee and hip-joint
angling out of his parchment skin.
He was still and silhouette-black;
even his eyes didn't move as I ran in.
Mother, churning her butter-milk,
asked me to give him a tumbler.
Gingerly I held out a clay urn
lest our fingers touched.
He drank and left, soundless,
a vision creeping away
from a hardening eyeball.

Later there were thousands;
footsore hordes scouring the land for forage,
numerous enough to start a tiger-beat
in every *nullah*. And herds,
first camels and then goats
which hugged the stems with forepaws
and nibbled away, till the trees
were left only with a green head of hair.
Well, the wheel's come full circle, as they say.

Do you see trains steaming out,
ten thousand frying on the lurching roofs?
It is our carts rolling today,
our villages walking out with their headloads,
an ant-line following
the scent of a moist root.

---

nullah: stream, watercourse, ravine.
Author's note: Like 'Calendar Starting June', 'Migrations' is also a poem on
the drought of 1979 – I accompanied the Prime Minister on his inspection
tours of the affected areas in Madhya Pradesh (the old Central Provinces) and
Uttar Pradesh, (UP as it is commonly known). Formerly, people from Rajasthan,
which boasts of a considerable desert, used to migrate to UP. This particular
year (1979) it was the other way around.

The Magician's Son

A jackdaw may smile but the magician's son
will not utter a word. The dandruff of expression

has been blown from his eyes.
He never smiles and he never cries.

His father holds his thistle-thin arms shoulder-high and wide
like the wings of a dying heron on his final glide.

Every day the same routine,
the traffic of the boy's mind

halted by the father's hands, the awareness kissed
away from the face by an occult mist.

On an upthrust sword-point they make him lie supine.
Why doesn't the sword-blade enter the spine

of this senseless huddle, rigid from knee to throat?
The sword removed, he levitates, he floats

for some hypnotic moments, and dares
gravity, asleep on a hammock which isn't there.

They have to bring him back, they have to bring him back!
Anton Mesmer himself leads the attack.

Much waving of arms, intensely focused eyes!
He comes back, the mists exorcized.

Some black tide, oil-polluted, has left him on the beach,
this coastal bird, child-fish, in man's polluted reach.

He rises, walks, strains;
the drowned-bird look remains.

Where is the fantasy here, where the mantic spell,
wand and pentacle?' I asked, 'this is no magic, hell'.

As I drove back angry over Ameera Kadal
rain broke, white magic rain from the cloud's dark spell.

Ameera Kadal: a bridge over the river Jhelum in Srinagar, Kashmir. 'Kadal'
means 'bridge' in Kashmiri.

Crossing Chorhoti

These two days past we had left
the smell of mint behind us,
and thyme and bhojpatra trees
and Bhotiya children pouched
on the backs of their mothers,
luminous among black capes.

We had transcended already
the world of pollen and drifting spore,
the green congeries of moss and lichen
and the dark gods of fertility.
We were trekking past saw-toothed crags
touched with mineral oxides
and so wind-scarred that we called them
the rock-temples of Rimkhim.
The evening was beryl-blue
as we left the grass-bowl of Barahoti
and reached the wind shadow.
In a place which has no grass, no trees,
no dust, you cannot see the wind.

At 16,000 feet, near Bamjar,
we pitched our alpine tents.
Loose shale lay over the plain,
glinting in the last rays of the sun,
and bones so grey and leaden that diamonds
in their vicinity would have been dulled.
'Goats were slaughtered here, but why
in such numbers?' I asked my Bhotiya friend.
And Ran Singh answered, avoiding my eye,
'Some hundred Tibetans, a decade back,
were caught in a snowdrift and that was that.'
Suddenly the night grew teeth
and the wind became a switchblade.

Tibet was across,
the same sky covered us both.
The constellations over the Lamas

were the same as over us.
Once they may have rained peace
and the benediction of the Buddha,
but now they were cloven-footed,
boar-snouted and lion-maned,
aggressive drives of the gods
that went warring through the night.

Dreams came ghost-lit
and shortly guttered
like the butter-lamps of Tibet.
At four in the morning, when the constellations
still moved around us like the last
revolutions of a giant prayer-wheel,
we set off plodding,
eyes fixed on the next six feet.

It was a race against the wind gods;
we had to reach the pass
before the winds got there.
We crunched our way across the frosted earth
over the rock-and-bone tundra,
then up a defile on to a stretch
of gently rising rock.
We had transcended even moisture now,
the thin spread of frost was not there,
nor ice-ruts splintering under the feet like glass.

The deities here were rock and height,
not forgetting wind, for we were near the pass.
The winds came down like the shrill chant of women.
The winds howled like a hundred tantric gods.
Ran Singh came out with a Bhotiya proverb:
'They are tough alike, crossing a pass
or bearing a child!'

I have no curse nor mantra
to keep the demons from me.
I have no foolproof earplug
to keep wind-voices from me.
I am nearing the escarpment
where wrapped in fog she towers,
O mother-goddess Dolma,
symbol of the perfect flower,
brooding over my future
rock-ledges stand, like druids,
my blood congeals to frost-dust,
my bones are churned to fluid.
Breathe vowels through my spine-flue
to keep me poised and balanced,
to keep me moving towards
the axis of my being.

Goddess I am seeking shelter
from the approaching storm.
I seek the cavern-aspect
of your embracing form
which smothers in lap-darkness
yet lights the spinal reed.
From your womb all proceeded,
into you all recede.

The upper reaches of the pass were straight,
a vertical thrust that obscured the sun
and half the sky. Treading over grit
we felt the air-drifts quiver
as we touched the top ozone and ether,
and a shellburst of light greeted us
as fifty Indian peaks erupted
with snow and the spray-hangover
of icefalls and the blue of distance,
as if some god had with a palette-knife
honed the landscape with ethereal colours.

I recalled the Buddha's words and deflected them:
'Opened wide are the gates of immortality,
ye that have eyes to see release your faith.'

But irony haunted me even at this height;
Kailash was veiled by a cloud layer of white.

Chorhoti: a pass at 18,880 feet near the Indo-Tibet border, which the poet
crossed in 1964.

The Round of the Seasons
(In the footsteps of Abhinanda and Yogeswara)

Vasanta (Spring)

I tire of superstitions:
the asoka blossoms only
at the touch of the beloved's feet;
the bakula must be splashed
with rinsed wine from her mouth;
the tilaka must be hugged
and the amaranth should get a glance from her
before leaf turns green
or the petals colour.

I quicken into flower
at the memory of your touch.

2

It is the season for illusions:
night mists turn to dawn haze,
frost becomes dew, though sharp.
The night-jar still coughs.
The blackbird is heard sometimes
but she hasn't been seen.
The scent of the mango-blossom is there
but not the mango-blossom.
A bird alights on the leafing lotus bed
thinking it is an island.
Bathing on the ghats,
shawled in mist, she finds
bees moving towards her breast-tips.

GRISHMA (SUMMER)

Kama, in this torrid summer
let some things remain cool:
her eyes, reflecting the waters,
the smell of jasmine in her hair,
her body dripping with the cold river
as she steps out on the ghats.
If you need tapers at your altar, Kama,
let her ardour burn.
Let thoughts burn within the cool forehead.
Let the cheeks be cold
but the tongue within all fire.

2

From the mountain's shoulder to its groin,
from nether regions
to the lip of the escarpment,
forest fires rage simultaneously.
Bark and bud crackle and rain down as ash.
The trapped antelope does not know where to run
as the four directions, wrapped in smoke,
converge on him.
Such is my fate, beloved,
in the forest of your limbs,
under the black rain of your hair.

Author's note: Asoka, bakula and tilaka are flowers mentioned in old Sanskrit
verses. The celebrated author and translator Martha Selby writes: 'According
to Monier-Williams *asoka* is "the tree Jonesia Asoka Roxb. [a tree of moderate
size belonging to the leguminous class with magnificent red flowers]." *Bakula* is
"a kind of tree, Mimusops fElengi [said to put forth blossoms when sprinkled
with nectar from the mouths of lovely women]." *Tilaka* is "Clerodendrum
phlomoides [Symplocos racemosa]." '
Kama: the god of love in the Hindu pantheon.

A Take-off on a Passing Remark

Tall buildings impress me
   the ones which cut off half the sky.
I like tall stories, even though false;
   not the half-truth sleeping with the half-lie.
I want things on a large scale:
   amplitudes, a sense of space and light,
the great yellow eye of the train
   lighting up the distances of the night.
Urchins, furred caterpillars, moles
   and fern-beds are all right.
But I want flowering trees, long
   streamers of moss, flaming parasites.

But when you ask, still squirrel-young
   short as twilight
   short as a shadow at noon
why I love you, what can I answer?

Four for Ted Roethke

The Roethke family owned one of the biggest green-houses in America, a quarter of a million square feet under glass. Perhaps Theodore Roethke's deep involvement with nature stems from this background. 'The Father-florist' is a poem on his father Otto Roethke. The son's love for his father and the slights he suffered, slights which a boy of his excessive sensitivity could not forget, recur in his poems. So does Otto Roethke's death, which had a traumatic effect on the poet.

Roethke suffered his first mental disturbance in November 1935 at Michigan State College. As Alan Seager tells it in *Glass House* (McGraw Hill), his excellent biography of the poet, Roethke, in a rather curious sequence of events, started drinking heavily – whisky, beer, dozens of cups of coffee, and swallowing aspirin tablets by the handful. On 11 November 1935, while in this state, Roethke left his room in Campus Hotel and 'walked out to a stretch of woods on Hagedorn road'. While here, he told Peter de Vries later, he had a mystical experience with a tree and learned there the 'secret of Nijinsky.' In *The Diary of Vaslav Nijinsky* (Simon and Schuster, New York, 1936) the following passage occurs:

> I sat, I sat a long time, then I pretended to fall asleep- I pretended because I felt that way. Whenever I have a feeling, I carry it out. I never fight against a feeling… I went on and came to a tree. The tree told me that one could not talk here, because human beings do not understand feelings. I went on. I was sorry to part with the tree because the tree understood me (pp. 32-3).

It was a cold night and Roethke took off his shoes to circulate the blood in his freezing feet. He left the shoes there, walked several miles and hitched a ride back, after finding himself on the road to Owosso. He took a hot bath. Next morning he again went out for a walk, and when he landed in the Dean's office he was delirious.

In November 1949 he had another attack of 'hyperactivity and disorganized behaviour'.

Roethke's marriage to Beatrice O'Connell in January 1953, and a happy decade that followed, find mention in my last poem, 'The Season of Light'.

THE FATHER-FLORIST

The Father-florist holds the key;
he makes the rose and orchid pulse,
he brings a flush to canna's cheek,
quickens mildew, moss and scum.
He turns the heat on when he wants
makes steam-pipes and the greenhouse hum.

Humus and heat are what he gives
with one knob-turn to son and flower.
The vine or sapling of his choice –
he simply moves it from its spot
from outer fringes of the cold
to where the air is moist and hot.

Capilarious the winter sap
goes shooting up in branch and stem.
The steam goes up, knocking in pipes.
The father gets up now and then
at night to regulate the heat
and tend the pale-pink cyclamen,

and order his small universe,
the sweet-peas piled on wire and string,
full forty-seven metres high;
and tucked away, beyond the pale
in some vile corner, leaf-mould and manure,
grub and the forward-glistering snail.

The boy can help his father now,
he's old enough to pluck the weeds
that loll and flicker in the dirt
between the concrete flower-beds.
He's old enough to pluck the weeds,
he's old enough to feel the hurt.

Crawling on fours, tugging in dark
on bristly stem with bruised hands,
at one with smells of musk and slime,
while orchid, rose and carnation
are tended by the father, who
does not know he has lost a son.

GRASS AND WIND

An owl-hoot made the night darker.
Mice and worm kept the pebbles warm.
In the stillness he heard a flower
breathe; and sang
as over the iron-grey river
water birds rang.

Didn't hear ghosts whistle or trolls scream,
but heard fish breathe, lungs distended
without the hug of water.
The fish wants to talk, he told
Papa, don't thump it against the boat.
Papa threw it back among the shoals.

In a spray of memories
Papa was rainbow-god.
Then he fell like a shot crow.
Isn't around any more.
Went to the vale of dying birds,
to the creek of the dying roe.

He wished for his return
but Papa had gone. Prayer
unanswered led to loss of faith.
God was someplace else, perhaps within
an unknown cellar
or grotto of crumbling skin.

Walked from empty house to cave-door,
behind which there was nothing;
heard emptiness whine inside him.
His loneliness sensed
where the clouds came from
and where the roots went.

Leaking faucets talked rain.
He heard saplings grow, their joints
snap and crackle. He heard
what he wanted to, had no choice.
River and water rushes spoke alike,
grass and wind had the same voice.

BREAKDOWN

It was the dark way he took,
the one without doors,
as he walked out on himself.
Leaves did not mock him and stick out their tongues
for there were no leaves.
He prayed to snail and worm,

as he walked, stripped of sheath and habit,
disguise and subterfuge, ill-clad
to take the night's brunt. Something
was wrong with the season within.
Fire intrudes here, but his brain
was a wild fire looking for the wind.

All pasts are full of losses,
so was his. He recalled father's face
through glass-window coffin. Guilts, shames,
moles scurried as he moved in. That night
he walked into the woods
alone, where he encountered light

for a firefly-moment, or so
he thought. A feeling had carried him
towards this lambency.
He had followed without remonstrance
this feeling that he was love embodied,
that love itself was some sort of trance

in which the body intervened
and broke the spell.
Keeping the body away from love
is difficult at the best of times.
He beat back the flesh-fires, and froze.
He had come upon a cold clime.

Took off his shoes to circulate
the blood; thought he found the key
to Nijinsky who had come
upon a tree, the bark peeling,
which told the Russian not to talk there
for man does not understand feeling.

Already high on aspirin
and alcohol, he thought he saw
the light. Always the vase was tilted
not just for light but revelation.
If anything filled his urn, amphorae, vase,
it was hallucinations.

A poem like a river moves
from dark to light, a flow
his river was to find.
The ice-filmed waters in him cracked.
He came out shivering wet but whole;
he needed love, he needed time.

The Season of Light

Something dark and filmed with damp,
converse with pebble, root and dirt,
are things the dead find in a grave.
The grave and greenhouse were the same
for some dark moments. A light appeared,
a yellow flower squirted flame.

He ran his passions up the mast.
A breeze that came to Dante once
and left him stricken, came to him.
It found him vulnerable, bare.
Her hair took on the blaze of light,
wind took the colour of her hair.

A southern wind, it carried him
with bird and fish towards the north.
The star-wheel turned, he was on course.
The desolations now were gone.
Luxuriating in her flesh
vague stirrings of the soul were born.

Marrow and pulse beat wildly now.
Beneath their movements waters heaved.
But space, awhirl around them, stilled.
Both storm and stillness were the bride.
Their flesh-shoals rocked
to the spirit's tide.

An empathy with dark beginnings
moving to light took hold of him,
the stir of root and bug and snail,
mole-scribble on a text of moss.
It slowly trickled out of him
this sense of lostness and of loss.

He saw his image in another.
The carnal ghost had troubled him earlier on.
Longing and lust both went along
hand in hand. Earth, light and air
and bird and tree became one song.

He ordered his small universe
of loam and memory, sun-through-glass.
Frost paved it with its morning breath.
(Inside creation seethes and yeasts.)
Later in day light came and knocked:
Eternity was manifest.

from
A SUMMER OF TIGERS

The Glass-Blower

He knew about glass and its history;
beads of the vintage of Amenhotep;
the Niniveh tablets of Assurbanipal;
blowpipe, marver, pontil, each successive step

Which fire took to make clay transparent.
'Glass is not in the family,' he said.
'My forefathers were alchemists, sublimators
of baser alloys like zinc and lead;

believers in a four-cornered universe
of water and air, earth and fire.
They spent a lifetime with bellows, furnaces.
They were metallurgists, but they aspired

to mysticism. Alchemy for them was not
some quack technique harnessed to greed of wealth.
The goal was transmuting the earthy
into the celestial, sickness into health.

Now things are changed; a philosophy slips out
as an age loses its teeth. Nothing holds fast.
Decay sets in with birth:
we rust like iron, we splinter like glass.'

2

We walked past litter to his boiler room
where a reed-thin boy in a tattered vest
and a lost face dipped his blowing iron
into a small vat of silica paste.

The furnace, fitted with fire-clay pot and flue,
crackled and hissed. The stilt legs of the boy
glowed faint red on the shin-bone as he put
the blowing iron to his lips and blew.

His cheeks turned to hemispheres, fully blown.
His neck, corded and veined, struggled up to the nape
with his exhalations. A blob ballooned
at the pipe's other end and froze into shape.

A smell of burnt resin, fossil gum, miracles,
of just fallen lightning came from the bowl,
as it should, with clay altered to replicate
the luminous transparencies of the soul.

The first time men saw this state of mist,
this veil that veiled nothing – O glorious deception –
and glass cool into colour of space, did they cry out
'This is no object, it is thought, perception!'

Childhood Poem
For A. K. Ramanujan

There's precious little to a childhood once
you've forgotten it. One can probe no further.
In limbo , one absence, one vacancy
is as good as another.

'Why can't you remember?' my wife asks, 'I can.'
I do not answer, wish to avoid friction.
I couldn't be unique in my forgetfulness –
childhood is a fairly common affliction.

My few memories are of Lyallpur,
now Faizalabad, named after the king.
If Idi Amin had signed a large enough cheque
they would have named this dustbowl after him.

First memories: dust storms I can still taste, one mulberry tree
in whose dark shadow we gorged on fruit.
I don't recall kites, spinning tops, birds;
no other tree, nor trunk nor branch nor root.

Sacred Hearts school and Italian fathers,
bald bearded, stout.
War made them prisoners of war. When they stitched
the school up with barbed wire, Father pulled me out.

Arya School; God save us from the Aryans.
Boys spilled in from an orphanage nearby
with pockmarked faces and purple splotches.
'Sing'. I sang 'London Bridge is falling down'.
The refrain 'My fair lady', they thought was obscene
and reached, (thank God) for their own respective crotches.

We sat on jute strips spread out on the grass,
a *takhti* resting on the right thigh;
dipped our quills in clay inkwells and set out
on the seas of Urdu calligraphy.

113

The pen was no wand, instead of the rondures
and scimitar curves of the Urdu alphabet
I produced serrations and smudges,
charred centipedes on a wooden slate.

When the Master wanted sleep he shouted 'Tables!'
We learnt them by rote in an endless choric drone.
It was not memorizing but amnesia.
I would nod into sleep without a groan.

The Master, Chaitandev, wore *turra* and turban.
You could play golf with his eyeballs, grotesquely askew.
When you thought he was looking the other way
you fell in his distorted line of sight. He had you

by the wrist, gave it a corkscrew turn
and rammed his fist in the pith of your back.
You threshed the floor gasping for some moments
and then flopped inert like an empty sack.

Kanwar Ram replaced him, he wore salwars
wide enough to have blocked the road.
Strong in his biceps and arithmetic
the replacement didn't bode me any good.

My iron slate had shed its frame. As I assailed
him with my scrambled digits I could feel
his anger and fled. The slate hurled like a flail,
severed flesh and tendon, an inch above my heel

and laid me low for a week.
One other memory lingers –
a swooping kite that makes off with
a crumb of bread from between my fingers.

I was taken piggyback to watch *mohorram*
streaming down the radials to the Gol Bazar.

114

A clutch of chained knives played a jingle on their backs.
The dead saints saw to it they left no scar.

Two years before Muslims asked for another country
the way you reach out for another piece of bread
we left Lyallpur for Junagadh.
Left two brothers behind, now one of them is dead.

They went through hell, that is Punjab, Sindh, Rajputana;
showing sacred threads each time to prove a different case:
not Hindu first, not Muslim later. One took shelter
in a brothel – lucky guy, I wish I were in his place.

But what they told me then is vivid still.
The summer of 1947:
a sabre procession two miles long, blue-robed Nihangs
and an overhang of dust like a scourge from heaven.

The procession snaking like a turban unwound.
Fiery slogans, sabres drawn:
'Akhand rahega Hindustan!
Nahin banega Pakistan'.

But I wasn't there. The procession for me
was a string of long-robed spear-headed words.
What can one say when simulacra turns vivid
and the real gets blurred?

Beyond this I recall nothing
the gates of memory have been closed.
Sometimes I mourn for this loss of faces;
that haunted past, now sadly devoid of ghosts.

---

takhti: a big wooden slate on which you learn writing in Urdu.
turra: a conical cap around which the Punjabi turban is wound.
mohorram: the first month of the Muslim year. The first ten days of the month are observed in mourning for the martyrdom of Husain, the second son of Ali and Fatimah.
'Akhand rahega Hindustan! / Nahin banega Pakistan': 'India will remain one! / Pakistan will not be formed.'

115

The Poseidonians
After Cavafy

> [We behave like] the Poseidonians in the Tyrrhenian Gulf, who
> although of Greek origin, became barbarized as Tyrrhenians or
> Romans and changed their speech and the customs of their
> ancestors. But they observe one Greek festival even to this day,
> during this they gather together and call up from memory their
> ancient names and customs, and then lamenting loudly to each
> other and weeping, they go away.
>
> Athenios, *Deipnosophistai*, Book 14, 31A [632]

All it takes to blight a language
is another sun. It's not burn
that does it, or chill, or the way
woods straggle down the hills, or seas
curl along the shingled coast.
It is the women, cowering
in fear, whom the soldiers,
as they clamber down the boats,
first reassure and then marry.

They are faithful, good with grain,
at baking bread and fermenting wine
and unscrambling the fish shoals from the meshes.
They get the goddesses wrong sometimes [but so what?]
confusing mother with daughter.
And there are minor errors
in ritual and sacrifice,
in lustration oils and libations.

A few seasons teach the man
that his woman's omen birds are always right;
her fears travel down the bloodstream
and a new language emerges from the placenta.

What does one do with a thought
that embarks on one script and lands on another?
A hundred years go by, perhaps two hundred,
living with the Tyrrhenians and the Etruscans,

and they discover there is more to language
than merely words, that every act
from making wine to making love
filters through a different prism of sound,
and they have forgotten the land they set sail from
and the syllables that seeded that land.

What do they do, except once a year
at a lyre-and-lute festival,
Greek to the core, with dance and contests,
grope for memories in the blood,
like Demeter, torch in hand,
looking for her netherworld daughter?
And weep a little for the Greece they have lost
and reflect on the gulf of years which has proved
wider than the Tyrrhenian gulf,
and the hiatus between languages
wider than the Aegean?
What can they do, but weep for Agora
and Acropolis, for ever left behind;
and reflect, how three centuries distant
from the Ionian coast,
they have been barbarized by Rome?

A Tale of Two Statues

Once the tar brush was out
on the slogan-streets
they shifted Victoria to the Police Lines.

There's nothing shamefaced about her,
as she stands under the neem,
imperial and abdominous,
dust wedged in the folds
of her bronze robes,
her tiara caked with bird-lime.

But at her feet there are flowers.
Women think she is Devi.

At first sight
revolutionaries ran
jubilant, shouting
'Bowled! Bowled!'
as under the pedestal
Gandhi's clay head rolled.

---

neem: a tree in the mahogany family.
Author's note: this poem was written in the 1970s when 'Naxalites' were
decapitating Gandhi's statues. It was first published by Syd Harrex in his book
Only Connect.

from
NIGHT RIVER

Living on Hyphens

Living on hyphens
a man needs to anchor himself.
Between dream and landscape
and between dream and the dark blood
congealing on cobblestones;
between hierarchy and disorder;
between the slow rhythms of seasons
and the frenetic pace of blood;
a man must arrive
at some sort of understanding.

Some people are lucky:
they function under two skies;
a sky of feeling
for each dialect of love
they instinctively possess;
and a different sky of history
over each separate past.

Between the face and the mask
that looks better than the face;
between love for the land
and hatred for the times;
between the smog one lives in
and the hope one lives on;
a man, a woman
must come to an understanding.

But happiness lies in the familiar,
in the penumbra one can sense.
Not soot from the heavens, necessarily
and the grit-encrusted air –
but yesterday's blue space still pulsing
with yesterday's light and radio signals.
Happy with just one boxed-in sky,
one feeling – love,
one sense – of loss,
one window – despair.

Bird Eclipse

Birds know an eclipse from a cloud;
                    we've all learnt that.
When moisture shades the sun
                    they don't turn silent.
In fact bird-calls seem to trigger
                    black nimbus into rain.
But when a planet intervenes
                    and turns silhouette,
Its dark rim bristling
                    with fire-lit stakes
They scurry into shrub and leaf
                    and bird-heavy tree;
Clamber into long
                    tendrillous vine
And turn deathly quiet
                    like children cowering
As father enters
                    blind with drink.

Epitaph for a Spanish Peasant
After Paul Eluard

Franco enlisted me and so I fought.
I did not desert: I was afraid I'd be shot.
While in the army I was gripped by fright:
So I battled against liberty, justice, right,
Under Irun's walls along with shell, shrapnel, flame.
And death caught up with me all the same.

Barracks Version

When Franco enlists you, you bloody well fight;
or he puts a bullet up your arse – get me mate!
So I didn't desert. My ruling star was fear.
I bayoneted liberty – you guessed it – in the derriere,
all under Irun's walls.
And still, and still death got me by the balls.

Contradictory You

You are
where the waters are
and the rain is
and ferns that fan out.
You are
where the vegetable dyes are
where colours are a dialect
and the dark is a language.

You are
where no subterfuge is.

You are
where the shadows are
lined under the eyelids.

You are
where the night is,
grained with the milky way
and granuled with stars.

You are
where the flicker and spray
of light and waterfall are.

You are the wharf
where my ship is berthed.
You could be the rock
where my ship is wrecked.

You are
where mirrors are
and memory is.
Memory is just a mirror
of your body's flank.

You are
where the sculptures are,
muslin-folds draped
over slim girdle and heavy hip.

You are
where the blue trance of the mountain is
and the fever of the valley.
You are
where the night was.
You are
where the rain-rinsed morning is.

The Stalin Epigram

The land speaks to us and we cannot hear
Unheard from ten paces, words disappear.

The one we hear about is the Kremlin mountaineer,
The assassin, and peasant-slayer.

His ten fingers are thick, grub-fat, great.
His words are iron measures of dead weight.

Roaches laugh on his upper lip and face,
The gleam on his boot tops cannot be effaced.

Half-men are mirrored in that shining boot rim,
Chicken-necked genuflectors who've surrounded him.

One caws, another meows, one scrapes like a broom,
He points his forefinger as he prates and booms.

The anvil is littered with his horse-shoes and decrees,
One each for the eyes, groin, forehead and the knees.

Like berries he rolls executions on his tongue,
He could hug his victims like old friends from home.

'The Stalin Epigram': an oft-translated poem of Osip Mandelstam. The next two poems ('Poem 8' and 'By the River Kama') are poems taken out of a section of ten poems entitled 'Stalking Mandelstam'. In both these poems the poet is addressing Mandelstam through his own poems.

Poem 8

Not quietly,
not like walking out of an old song,
or moving into the dark speech of silence,
did I leave.

The moment of metal arrives:
clang of wheel on rail,
the roll and reverberation
of steel on steel;
the first jab of the piston,
       the serrating lurch
of the panting engine;
steam-hiss
condensing to low cloud
       in cold air.

North is the home of exile,
home of the North wind
which can brook no walls.
A man, a woman, three soldiers
moving north
under a three-year iron sentence:
'isolate and preserve!'

Don't they see something strange here,
       something unseemly?
a man, a woman being herded
into some kind of frosted hell
where rats scurry and floorboards creak
and the state's executioners
are let loose on the wilderness?
Yet not one person on the swarming railway stations,
not one of the half-starved men,
huddled in cattle trucks that pass us by,
not one co-passenger on the river steamer
       looks us in the eye.

Knowing what is coming
is worse than not knowing it.
To look for a specific sound
in the journey's clamour –
the click of a bolt pulled back –
is worse than the bolt actually snapped back.
  Where are they going to shoot me?
  Here in the train,
  or the river-steamer?

That man in the red shirt
who boards the train with an axe,
  is he going to behead me?
The voices are around me,
and I don't know from where they emerge.

Five sleepless nights and then she slept,
leaving me to my
hospital bed in Cherdyn,
listening to my silence.
Instinct woke her up,
or a click of an insect that
  defined the long night of the Urals,
and she found me at the window-edge,
  grabbed my jacket,
as I wriggled out of the sleeves and fell
two floors below, but on ploughed up earth.

The long nights of the Urals,
sidereal in expanse.
The white nights of the Urals;
night smeared with rain,
rain smeared with the night.
The first ice sketched upon the winter floor;
I find myself mirror-meditating,
and move, only to hear
my image rustle under the ice.

By the River Kama

Along the Kama, darkness has its home.
Beside it, you think, cities pray on their knees.

Both noon and vesper under an unlit dome,
as shawled in mist, the bearded black firs ease

into their reflections. Fatigued in body, soul, you brim
with apprehension. You think of slaves and galleys

as they row you down to Kazan and Cherdyn.
While oar and image erase each other as they please.

River-watch, reverie; mid-stream you think of flight;
your window curtain billows as the wind blows hard.

You land on reality: the wife's five sleepless nights,
as she keeps watch over watchmen and the guard.

from
THE MAP-MAKER

Old Map-maker
For Felipe Fernandez-Armesto

True, map-makers from Majorca are small.
We're not from Andalusia or Portugal;
have no crusading experience
like that man with a name
long enough to crawl around a wall:
Gadifer de la Salle,
who conquered islands, looking for
'rivers of gold'. Or that Peraza family
of Seville, seeking the sources,
not of rivers, but slaves.

We were keen on star-bearings,
latitudes, distances. Trade routes
and sea-lanes were our companions,
and the extremities of winds
as they flopped on still seas.

Map-makers from a place as small
as Majorca should be quiet, they said.
Their tall stories should be short.
Symbols on their charts must be
the thing itself and not the mask.
Don't bring in all those great black kings –
there weren't any. Don't arm them
with sceptre and orb in your spurious maps –
they won't know what the damned things mean.

They were wrong.
It wasn't just the sea-lanes that we mapped.
We drew even veins of gold along our charts.
The world's richest place
was in the African interior,
between the Sahara
and the rain forest, dark as cumulus,
between the brown savannahs
and the grey scrub of the Sahel.
Yes, the kingdom of Mali, it was called.

Its location, a secret kept from all,
even those who traded gold
with the caravans, as they crossed the Sahara
towards the Mediterranean.

Ibn Batuta proved us right later.
But our brother cartographers
from Genoa and Venice scoffed at us.
How can I tell them that
scale has nothing to do with it?
We may be tiny, but perspectives
lean out of islands and voyage on.

But gold was not what I wished to talk of.
Star-bearings, latitudes,
trade routes enthralled us,
and conceiving the boundaries
of inconceivable distance.

Agni Sutta
(The Fire-Sermon)

That day as you set out for Uruvela
with the first birdcalls, things seemed just right.
You moved like a benediction over the land.
They flocked to your side, disciple, anchorite
and disbeliever; the procession grew
as we moved on – Gaya was our goal.
People lined the road, waiting to pour
their faith and fervour in each begging bowl.

Even on a road life plays itself out:
a bird cried out in agonized distress.
We passed a haze of lamentation
over a burning ghat; even we felt stressed.
Then a village feasting around a temple gong –
a child-monk had been tonsured, him the Buddha blessed.

At Gaya, Lord, we thought you'd skip the sermon.
Dusk had fallen, it was getting late.
We got a mouthful instead and wondered later
if it was that bird crying for its lost mate
which had upset you. Your pace was swift,
your glowing countenance just a fraction stern.
And when you spoke of the ear on fire and sound on fire
and the tongue on fire, on which words fry and burn,
we sensed trouble. It was not your usual lecture
on illusion in which we are all mired.
'The eye O priests is on fire,' you continued,
'forms are on fire, eye-consciousness is on fire.'
And you talked of thirsts on fire and things intangible
        on fire –

that evening everything seemed to be in flames.
'The mind is on fire, mind-consciousness is on fire
and sensations are on fire, the ones you claim
are yours.' And how are these on fire, you asked
and answered that in your own fashion.
'With the fires of hatred and infatuation' you said;
'with birth, old age and sorrow, with the fire of passion.'

But you missed the fire of absence, Lord,
and absence is an eternally empty bowl,
except for flame and sorrow feeding on each other.
The fire in human voids, who can these control?
You missed this particular fire, Lord!
And somehow my mind wandered to the bird cry
and the fire of absence, that burns a hole
in the soul, the heart, drills a hole in the sky.

Author's note: Gautam Buddha's Fire Sermon, was delivered in Gaya. 'Then the
Blessed One, having dwelt in Uruvela as long as he wished, proceeded on his
wanderings in the direction of Gaya Head, accompanied by a great congregation of
priests, a thousand in number, who had all of them aforetime been monks with
matted hair...' (Translated from 'Maha-Vagga' (p. 351), from *Buddhism in
Translations* by Henry Clarke Warren, National Banarsidas Publishers).
'Sutta' also appears as 'Sutra' and 'Agni Sutta', as 'Agni Sutra', 'Sutta' being
the Buddhist form of 'Sutra'.

Roof Observatory

He moved past the slab of damp air over damp ground,
past the two whining hinges of the rusted gate,
past rows of eucalypti with black leaves
and white leaves – moon on one, moon-shadow on the other;
past the duplicate patios, on to the double stairs
and into the hall of mirrors where he found himself
infinitely mirrored in a still moment of receding reflections.
Then on to the circular antechamber
with only himself and his shadow in attendance
to the roof where the double desolation of the garden
and the circular silence of the villa interior
sank into him like nightwaters filling up a forgotten tank;
till stepping on to a ladder, bone and ladder creaking,
he climbed into the quiet of his observatory;
where the solitudes were so large
that all else diminished in scale,
where the telescope hummed with planets
and the firmament fermented with astral fires,
and the glass lid on the barrel
multiplied the black spaces between the stars;
where at last, he thought, he was at one with,
and yet confronting, the universe.

But even there, Borges, the universe of your mind
was as large as the universe you were looking into.

Mirror Poem

1

Where the corridor
               is dark
the mirror cannot
retaliate with light.

Where the corridor
              is endless,
the mirror in the corridor
              is endless.

2

Space is depth.
A blue mirror lying on
              its back
looking up at the sky
throbs with space.
Looking down
              this vista
from the precipice of light
the hawk and the wheeling sky
move into vertigo.

Ruminating on the Galaxies
(Ramblings)

Are divides disappearing?
Are walls coming down?
Is time coeval with space?
Is space curved and round?
Foreground is all there is;
the background unknowable, lost.
How do you get to the past
under two millenniums of frost?

There are more worrisome things, Horatio,
than how astrology lied,
or how Buddhism, through its physics of karma,
disappeared from India and died
on the Indo-Gangetic plain,
in the very land of its birth.
Or how hieroglyphs withered,
sandpapered into the earth.
Or how Sanskrit, the mother of language
shrivelled, though with ne'er a flaw,
and was cremated alone, abandoned
by all her daughters-in-law.

Cosmologies died rather slowly,
in an age that saw no give and take;
where the word of the scripture was law
and heresies sizzled at the stake.
All bodies rotated around us –
that's how the Lord had willed it.
A cosmology started fading,
even as Copernicus killed it.

Where a quasar out-weighs a galaxy
and gravity makes light bend,
normal questions become irrelevant:
did the universe begin, will it end?

Century-end Prayer

Let the arctic birds,
friendly with polar winds,
have an easy time of it, Lord,
for the next hundred years.
I don't even know
if there *are* any arctic birds.
I am as ignorant
about bird-life near the Poles
as birds are about good and evil.
I wish my ignorance could also be
equated with innocence.

But my prayers are not hooked
to some mariner's compass;
and when I start walking down
with my back to the Pole Star,
I lead my prayers by the hand.
And here in warm-rain country
let the rhinoceros
trundle through mire
and the next millennium
and the next.
May the beaver and the porcupine
burrow their way
to their underground haven
and may the elephant shed his tusks
so that we don't shed his blood.

And a small skylight prayer, Lord:
may the sparrow know glass
from the crisp air outside.

New Poems

To a Palestinian Poet

You claim your vineyard has been robbed.
If the vineyard is robbed, then the wine is theirs.
If the wine is theirs, so is the intoxication.
But then what are you left with, without
vineyard, wine and intoxication?

You were born east of Acre in Galilee.
You were a kid in 1948.
In your innocence you are still a child,
railing against your destiny,
against the pitiless heavens –
in Urdu the sky, or *falak*, is always pitiless;
I don't know how it goes in your language.

Your destiny had a travel pass
which took you to unknown lands;
(unknown in the sense that you looked
for your home there and didn't find it).
The years had nothing much to teach you,
for you knew already that it's not just the desert
that can destroy your vineyards – history also can.

Your chant was exile
your blood was exile, your bread was exile.
I can see your blood curdle and turn thick
as Turkish coffee when you think of exile.

As a fellow poet I condone your excesses –
'measuring the sky with chains'…
'a blood drop looking for a wound.'
Let's have less of blood,
both in poetry and on the ground.

Let peace descend on you and your neighbouring people.
They too have had a two thousand year old exile.
I pray that they never drive your children into the desert
and may your children never drive them into the sea.

(*Damascus, 14 May, 2004*)

143

By-pass

1

Now I look for a by-pass everywhere –
the black serpent, well-tarred, leaving town
after a mere show of circumambulation,
sliding along the curve and yet not fully round;
leaving the city, shuttered with dogma,
its pretences wafer-crisp, slowly peeling;
leaving those wise counsels behind, 'Gather
yourself, get a hold over your feelings.'

'Look eastwards when you pray' (what makes them think I do?)
and such injunctions from adherents of the text.
(I can't think of directions, I only think of you).
There are others, well meaning, less circumspect
who say give rein to your feelings. I smile;
I'd unfurl my passions were there any left.

2

Hence cautiously, in the middle lane, between
demonology and miracle, both whizzing past,
I drive, yet unsure if I've broken away
and am moving into loneliness at last.
When you can't face up to dust and people
and memory that stalks you, this could mean flight.
Greater people have moved into ashrams, cults
and things, so why should I be denied

a change of course,
and this sudden hold on the suddenness of grief?
If the lease on faith is over, why the remorse?
And yet, this always happens, for a brief
moment the rear-view mirror confounds:
are you moving into or out of unbelief?

144

3

Moving into the open as villages fly past:
mud and tethered cows and hills of stacked grain;
moving, flanked by the seasons – mustard flower and wheat,
or was it earlier – cornstalk and rain?
Moving out has a good bit of illusion:
you think you are drifting towards solitudes.
Things gather here too, toll barriers, octroi posts
and spice-reeking *dhabas* strung with pin-up nudes.

And my shadow is the same everywhere
and that itself can sometimes be a crowd.
Though of this I am often unaware.
There's your shadow too, owing no allegiance to the sun.
Then fading light, this black serpent that I ride,
isn't it another name for oblivion?

4

It is the past you fear, loved body, image
and loved voice resurrected are what you dread.
And you will think of what was said that day
or not, and hence will now remain unsaid.
If all you wish to curve past is memory, take stock.
The past is mottled all over on the skin.
How do you slough it off? There's nothing
it hasn't colonized outside you or within.

So you turn the ignition, hoping to jolt the car
into action. The doubt-motor sputters:
the near doesn't mirror as much as the far.
Are you dazed or is reality askew? You don't know,
and even as you press the accelerator,
what if you discover there's nowhere to go?

5

A wayside *Fakeer* attracts me; I stop the car.
He talks of impermanence (the East's strong suit),
notes that sadness sits on me like a scar.
I buy a cup of tea, I offer him some fruit.
If you meditate on transience, life seems too long.
His answer is brief; for terseness you can't match it:
transience is a thought that comes to mind
and slips away before memory can catch it.

I try my hand at counselling myself
and explore the fog at the edge of things:
(tough at the best of times, these are the worst).
"Separation is a drifting into, not a guillotine."

A woman comes, head bowed, to the Fakeer.
She's pregnant, smiles, and leaves a bowl of *kheer*.

6

When light refracts, which light-sliver to follow?
Confusions don't end here, they're also there within.
How do I transport this baggage, and where –
all that yearning and lament bricked in?
Sheering off from nightmare, how does one steer
through a normal world? Insects and haze seem
to crowd the headlights. I don't know if I
am driving through twilight or a half-lit dream.

Distinctions fall like gnats, one may or may not know
light from Ahriman-dark, but illusions I define:
don't dream of elsewheres – there's no elsewhere to go.
A truck, coming from the other side, blinks
its one Cyclopean eye. One moves into the future,
even as it closes in.

---

ahsram: a hermitage.
dhaba: a cheap roadside eating house.
kheer: a sweet made of milk and rice.
Ahriman: Satan in Persian lore and the Zoroastrian religion.

We the Kauravas

We are the Kauravas, though we don't know why.
Father was blind and mother willed herself
into blindness with a band across the eyes.
As metaphors go, you can't beat that, can you?
Leaves you free to sink into any old manhole
left open by the municipality.

The other guys just asked for five villages;
some measly thatch huts, a few cows munching away
at the stubble and perhaps a tethered goat or two;
and the usual paraphernalia, detritus –
cattleherds to graze their cows, barbers
to shave armpits, faces and other places,
kahars for the palanquins when their girls
set out for the marriage bed.
That's all they wanted, though they ended up
edging us out of hearth and kingdom
and weeping over our bloodied corpses.

We shall always be the Kauravas, mind you,
nothing will change that.
Dusk will fall earlier for us, *godhuli*
or no *godhuli* (which if I may translate
for Stephanians and anglicized folk, means 'cowdust').
Someone will cry out "Ashwathama is dead,"
and we'll return our arrows to the quiver
till we are shot. All that'll happen to them is
that a chariot flying a foot above the earth
will suddenly be grounded – big deal!
And if *our* chariot gets stuck in the mud,
they'll be quick on the draw like some baddie
hamming his way in a B-grade Western.

They had a God-man too.
He tattooed his body completely blue.
He had an air conditioned ashram at Mathura.
If he as much as sneezed
they took him to Apollo or Batra.
And while we bled in battle and died, he gave
endless lectures on truth and righteous action,
all the while teaching our enemies how to kill us.

Yet we are the villains; the Kauravas
can't be anything else – we'd lose our part in the play!
But why are we the Kauravas, why didn't
the mantle of the pure fall across our shoulders?
Did we get the wrong tailors, Nathu?
or the wrong make-up 'artist', Lallu?
Why should we get shot or run over
and torn from the ones we love?
Must be fate and pre-natal karma.

On the other bank of transmigration,
as we brought our water buffaloes across,
we must have blundered upon some goddess
during her dawn bath or blackened
some pure water urn with our shadow.

Kauravas: the antagonists of the Pandavas in the Mahabharata.
kahars: a caste which lifts the palanquin in which the bride is seated as she
departs for her husband's house.
Ashwathama: a hero who fought for the Kauravas in the Mahabharata war.
Yudhishtir falsely declared that Ashwathama had died. As a result, his chariot,
which always floated a foot above the earth, was grounded.
Apollo and Batra: two very sophisticated hospitals in Delhi.

149

Invocation

We who write in asura nagari
in the land of the devas
We who write in the asura script
in the land of the devas
We, who parrot a language
that came across the black waters,
and scrambled our caste,
so that no one could help us,
not even the devas,
where shall we go from here?

We don't even know how to address you?
I must take recourse
to the sumptuous Tagorean phraseology,
and call you The Endless One,
for at symposia,
or at colloquia
thou art unending.
Forgive the odd line
where I use 'thee' and 'thou' and 'thine'
(these Nineteenth-century pearls
thrown in Twentieth-century slime).

You who live in the nest
woven by the south winds,
you whose name is warbled
by birds with scintillating wings
in sandal wood groves, hear us!
Literary Pope, we await your encyclicals.
(Those who protest, who accuse you
of thumping platitudes and harrumphing harangues,
we despise.) Savant of the East, arise!
Send your papal bulls into our cow belt –
and watch the rutting.

Light the way for us with your torch.
Tell us which doctor
will plant the gland of nativism
in our benighted souls.
Teach us how to distinguish between night and day.
Endless one, anantha,
show us the way!

---

asura nagri: there is no such word, but the script for Hindi, Sanskrit, Prakrit is called devnagari, the script of the Devas, or gods. Asurs are demons.

Biographical note

KEKI N. DARUWALLA is one of India's leading English-language writers. Born in 1937 in Lahore, he holds a Masters degree from Government College Ludhiana. He has published nine volumes of poetry, the fifth of which, *The Keeper of the Dead*, won him the Sahitya Akademi Award in 1982 and the sixth, *Landscapes*, the Commonwealth Poetry Prize for Asia in 1987. His *Collected Poems 1970-2005* appeared from Penguin India in 2006. He is also the author of three volumes of short stories, a novella, two collections of poetry for children and, most recently, *Riding the Himalayas* (2006), a unique travelogue of a car-trek by the author and twelve others from the Siachen Glacier in Ladakh to the easternmost tip of the Himalayas. He is also well-known as a writer on international affairs and a prolific reviewer.

Keki Daruwalla joined Government service in 1958 and served for many years in the Indian Police Service. In 1974, he joined the Cabinet Secretariat, was appointed Special Assistant to the Prime Minister in 1979 and, in 1980, was part of the Commonwealth Observers' Group for the Zimbabwe elections. When he retired, he was Chairman, Joint Intelligence Committee.

He is a Parsi Zoroastrian.

Also available in the
ARC PUBLICATIONS
International Poets series

LOUIS ARMAND (Australia)
Inexorable Weather

DAVID BAKER (USA)
Treatise on Touch

DON COLES (Canada)
Someone has Stayed in Stockholm

ALISON CROGGON (Australia)
The Common Flesh

SARAH DAY (Australia)
New & Selected Poems

GAIL DENDY (South Africa)
Painting the Bamboo Tree

ROBERT GRAY (Australia)
Lineations

MICHAEL S. HARPER (USA)
Selected Poems

SASKIA HAMILTON (USA)
Canal

ALAMGIR HASHMI (Pakistan)
The Ramazan Libation

DENNIS HASKELL (Australia)
Samuel Johnson in Marrickville

DINAH HAWKEN (New Zealand)
Small Stories of Devotion

BRIAN HENRY (USA)
Astronaut
Graft

RICHARD HOWARD (USA)
Trappings

T. R. HUMMER (USA)
Bluegrass Wasteland

ANDREW JOHNSTON (New Zealand)
The Open Window

JOHN KINSELLA (Australia)
America (A Poem)
Lightning Tree
The Silo:
A PASTORAL SYMPHONY
The Undertow:
NEW & SELECTED POEMS
Landbridge:
ANTHOLOGY OF CONTEMPORARY AUSTRALIAN POETRY
ED. JOHN KINSELLA

ANTHONY LAWRENCE (Australia)
Strategies for Confronting Fear

THOMAS LUX (USA)
The Street of Clocks

J.D.McCLATCHY (USA)
Division of Spoils

TRACY RYAN (Australia)
Hothouse

MARY JO SALTER (USA)
A Kiss in Space

ANDREW SANT (Australia)
The Unmapped Page

ELIZABETH SMITHER (New Zealand)
A Question of Gravity

C.K. STEAD (New Zealand)
Straw into Gold
The Right Thing
Dog

ANDREW TAYLOR (Australia)
The Stone Threshold

JOHN TRANTER (Australia)
The Floor of Heaven